"What Did He Say?"

A Book about Quotation Marks

by Tessa Kenan
illustrated by Anthony Lewis

amicus readers 3

Say Hello to Amicus Readers.

You'll find our helpful dog, Amicus, chasing a ball–to let you know the reading level of a book.

1 Learn to Read
Frequent repetition, high frequency words, and close photo-text matches introduce familiar topics and provide support for brand new readers.

2 Read Independently
Some repetition is mixed with varied sentence structures and a select amount of new vocabulary words are introduced with text and photo support.

3 Read to Know More
Interesting facts and engaging art and photos give fluent readers fun books both for reading practice and to learn about new topics.

Amicus Readers are published by Amicus
P.O. Box 1329, Mankato, MN 56002
www.amicuspublishing.us

Illustrations by Anthony Lewis

Produced for Amicus by The Peterson Publishing Company and Red Line Editorial.

Editor Jenna Gleisner
Designer Jake Nordby

Printed in Malaysia
10 9 8 7 6 5 4 3 2 1

Library of Congress Cataloging-in-Publication Data
Kenan, Tessa.
 "What did he say?": a book about quotation marks / by Tessa Kenan ; Illustrations by Anthony Lewis.
   pages cm. -- (Punctuation Station)
 Summary: "Trey's friends keep misinterpreting his story of a new pet, as the characters learn how to correctly use quotation marks in a sentence"-- Provided by publisher.
  ISBN 978-1-60753-727-4 (library binding)
  ISBN 978-1-60753-831-8 (ebook)
 1. Quotation marks--Juvenile literature. 2. English language--Punctuation--Juvenile literature. I. Title.
  PE1450.K38 2015
  428.1'3--dc23
                                        2014045805

Punctuation marks help us understand writing. Quotation marks show when someone is talking. We place quotation marks around words that are spoken.

"I have something exciting to tell my friends at recess," said Trey.

"I got a dog!" Trey told Ahmed.

"What color is it?" Ahmed asked.

"He is brown with a white spot," said Trey.

At the slide, Ahmed told Jane about Trey's new pet.

"Trey got a frog!" Ahmed said. "It is white with a brown spot."

Jane shared the news with Mya.

"Trey got a brown log with white spots," said Jane.

After recess, Mya asked Trey, "Did you really get a log for a pet?"

"That is not what I said," said Trey. "Who said that?"

11

"Jane said you got a brown log," said Mya.

"That is not what I said! Let me write it down," said Trey.

"I got a dog. He is brown with a white spot."

"You can tell what I said because I used quotation marks," said Trey. "I put them at the beginning and end of what I said."

"Do you want to come meet my new dog after school?" asked Trey.

Remember to use quotation marks:

To show when someone is speaking:

"I have something exciting to tell my friends at recess," said Trey.

To show the exact words someone said:

Trey said, "I got a dog. He is brown with a white spot."